WHAT CAUSED THE WAR OF 1812?

Sally Senzell Isaacs

Crabtree Publishing Company

www.crabtreebooks.com

Author: Sally Senzell Isaacs
Editor-in-Chief: Lionel Bender
Editor: Simon Adams
**Publishing plan research
and development:**
    Sean Charlebois, Reagan Miller
    Crabtree Publishing Company
Project Coordinator:
    Kathy Middleton
Print coordinator: Katherine Berti
Photo research: Bridget Heos
Designer and Makeup: Ben White
**Production coordinator
and technician:**
    Margaret Amy Salter
Production: Kim Richardson
Consultants:
    Richard Jensen, Research
    Professor of History, Culver
    Stockton College, Missouri

    Ronald J. Dale,
    War of 1812 Historian,
    1812 Bicentennial Project
    Manager, Parks Canada

Photograph credits:
Alamy (North Wind Picture Archives): 6–7, 22, 25, 26, 30, 32; 15l
    (INTERFOTO), 21 (Photri Images), 23 (The Art Archive), 35
    (GL Archive)
Associated Press: cover
Library of Congress: 1 (LC-USZC4-12011), 4 (LC-DIG-ppmsca-24329),
    4–5 (LC-DIG-pga-02159), 10 (LC-DIG-ppmsca-04314), 12–13
    (LC-DIG-pga-03074), 13t (LC-USZC4-5256), 15r
    (LC-DIG-ppmsca-10741), 16 (LC-USZ62-111116), 18
    (LC-USZC2-2416), 18–19 (LC-DIG-pga-01891), 20t
    (LC-DIG-ppmsca-15715), 20b (LC-DIG-ppmsca-15715), 33
    (LC-USZC4-6235), 34–35 (LC-DIG-pga-03578), 36
    (LC-USZC4-5917), 40–41 (LC-USZC4-6893), 41 (LC-USZC4-1082
shutterstock.com: 3 (Wally Stemberger), 7 (Jeffrey M. Frank),
Topfoto (The Granger Collection): 11, 13b, 17, 27, 28, 29, 31, 38–39, 39r;
    24–25 (Lightroom photos)
Maps: Stefan Chabluk

Cover: A woodcut shows American sailors being forcibly taken for
    impressment into service in the British Navy before 1812.
Title page: George Washington arrives at Congress Hall,
    Philadelphia, for his inauguration as President of the
    United Sates on March 4, 1793.

Library and Archives Canada Cataloguing in Publication

Isaacs, Sally Senzell, 1950-
    What caused the War of 1812? / Sally Isaacs.

(Documenting the War of 1812)
Includes bibliographical references and index.
Issued also in electronic format.
ISBN 978-0-7787-7962-9 (bound).--ISBN 978-0-7787-7967-4 (pbk.)

    1. United States--History--War of 1812--Causes--Juvenile litera-
ture.2. Canada--History--War of 1812--Causes--Juvenile literature.
I. Title.II. Series: Documenting the War of 1812

E357.I83 2011   j973.5'2   C2011-905241-5

Library of Congress Cataloging-in-Publication Data

Isaacs, Sally Senzell, 1950-
    What caused the War of 1812? / by Sally Senzell Isaacs.
        p. cm. -- (Documenting the War of 1812)
    Includes bibliographical references and index.
    ISBN 978-0-7787-7962-9 (reinforced library binding : alk. paper) --
ISBN 978-0-7787-7967-4 (pbk. : alk. paper) -- ISBN 978-1-4271-8831-1
(electronic pdf) -- ISBN 978-1-4271-9734-4 (electronic html)
    1. United States--History--War of 1812--Causes--Juvenile literature.
    2. United States--History--War of 1812--Sources--Juvenile literature.
I. Title. II. Series.

E354.I83 2011
973.5'2--dc23   2011029838

Crabtree Publishing Company

www.crabtreebooks.com   1-800-387-7650

Printed in the U.S.A./102012/CJ20120907

Published in Canada
Crabtree Publishing
616 Welland Ave.
St. Catharines, Ontario
L2M 5V6

Published in the United States
Crabtree Publishing
PMB 59051
350 Fifth Avenue, 59th Floor
New York, New York 10118

Published in the United Kingdom
Crabtree Publishing
Maritime House
Basin Road North, Hove
BN41 1WR

Published in Australia
Crabtree Publishing
3 Charles Street,
Coburg North
VIC 3058

CONTENTS

This book includes images of, and excerpts and
quotes from, documents of the War of 1812. The
documents range from letters, posters, and official
papers to battle plans, paintings, and cartoons.

INTRODUCTION

War of 1812

There are many nicknames for the War of 1812:

"Mr. Madison's War"
"The War with No Winner"
"The Second War of Independence"
"The War of Faulty Communications"

The War of 1812 drew in three countries at a crucial time in their histories. The first country was Great Britain, one of the most powerful countries in Europe with many colonies all over the world.

The second country was the United States of America, a new nation just 36 years old. Before 1775, the United States had consisted of 13 colonies ruled by Great Britain. In 1783, the colonies won their independence from Great Britain after the American Revolutionary War (1775–1783). By 1812, the new country had grown into 18 states.

Canada was the third country involved in the War of 1812 although it was not a nation at the time. It was ruled by Britain and known as British North America. Although the United States declared war on Great Britain, many battles took place in the provinces of Upper Canada (now Ontario) and Lower Canada (now Quebec). Why did this happen? British North America shared its southern border with the United States. Therefore, after declaring war, the United States invaded Upper and Lower Canada, which were the British provinces that sat

Below: James Madison was president of the United States when the War of 1812 broke out.

just across the northern borders of the U.S. states of New York, Ohio, and the Territory of Michigan.

Mr. Madison's War

On June 1, 1812, the fourth president of the United States, James Madison, asked Congress to declare war on Great Britain. He felt it was the only way to stop Great Britain from interfering with U.S. merchant ships on the world's oceans. Madison was the first U.S. president to declare war. It was not a popular decision. In all three countries, many people disagreed with Madison. Whatever Britain had done, war was not necessary, they said.

During the war, Madison fled from Washington, D.C., when British soldiers invaded and burned the Capitol building, the Treasury building, the Library of Congress, and the President's House (which was later painted white to cover the burn marks and renamed the White House).

Below: In 1775, Americans who wanted independence from Britain raised a liberty pole to signal their claim to make their own laws and raise their own taxes. This upset the British king, George III.

Untimely ending

The war started in 1812, but the fighting did not stop until February of 1815. The Treaty of Ghent that ended the war was signed by British and Americans meeting in Ghent, Belgium, on December 24, 1814, but the war did not officially end until the treaty went to London to be signed by the British, and then to Washington, to be signed by the President. Travel was slower in those days, and it took weeks for ships to sail across the ocean from Great Britain to North America. As the treaty document was crossing the Atlantic Ocean, soldiers continued fighting. The famous Battle of New Orleans, for example, was fought in Louisiana two weeks after the treaty was first signed. The treaty was officially ratified by the U.S. Senate and President Madison on February 16, 1815.

Right: The U.S.S. *Constitution* can be visited today in Boston Harbor, Massachusetts.

Below: On August 19, 1812, U.S. sailors on the ship U.S.S. *Constitution* battled the British ship H.M.S. *Guerriere*.

By the time the war ended, 24,000 U.S., British, and Native North American people had been killed in battle or had died of disease. There was not much to celebrate. There was no clear winner of the war. Neither side won anything new. Even the problems on the seas, which started the war, had mostly faded away before the war ended.

Reminders of the war today
Today, the histories of the battles are preserved at a number of historic sites. In the United States, these include New Orleans, Louisiana; Plattsburgh, New York; and Baltimore, Maryland. In Canada, there are historic sites at such places as Toronto, Ontario; Allan's Corners, Quebec; and Niagara-on-the-Lake, Ontario. The War of 1812 is also remembered for inspiring Francis Scott Key to write the song that would become the national anthem of the United States of America, "The Star-Spangled Banner."

Theaters of War

During the War of 1812, battles were fought in three main areas or three "theaters of combat." In the north, U.S. troops invaded Upper and Lower Canada and were in turn attacked by British, Upper Canadian, and Native North American forces based in these provinces. Naval actions took place on the Great Lakes. In the east of the continent, British ships blockaded U.S. ports, and British troops attacked Washington, D.C., and Baltimore, and raided along the coasts of New England. In the south, fighting occurred in Mississippi, Florida, Alabama, and Louisiana. The final battle of the war was fought in Mobile, Alabama.

Below: A map shows the makeup of North America in 1812. The United States consisted of 18 states and a number of territories that had yet to be organized and admitted to the Union. What is now Canada consisted of seven British provinces and the western territory, and was called British North America.

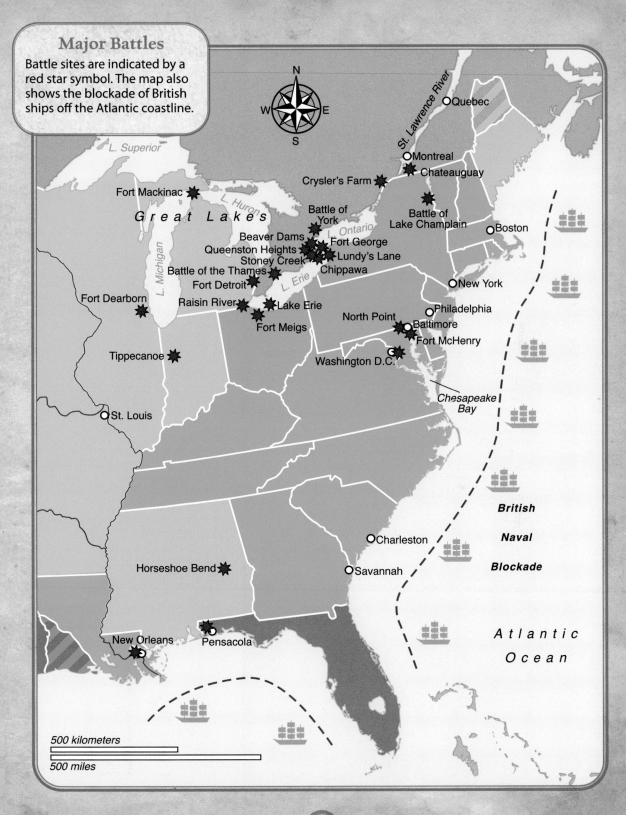

Major Battles

Battle sites are indicated by a red star symbol. The map also shows the blockade of British ships off the Atlantic coastline.

N W E S

Quebec

St. Lawrence River

Montreal

Crysler's Farm

Chateauguay

L. Superior

Fort Mackinac

L. Huron

G r e a t   L a k e s

Battle of York

Battle of Lake Champlain

Boston

Beaver Dams

L. Ontario

Fort George

Queenston Heights

Lundy's Lane

Stoney Creek

Chippawa

New York

Battle of the Thames

L. Erie

L. Michigan

Fort Detroit

Philadelphia

Fort Dearborn

Raisin River

Lake Erie

North Point

Baltimore

Fort Meigs

Fort McHenry

Washington D.C.

Tippecanoe

Chesapeake Bay

St. Louis

British

Charleston

Naval

Horseshoe Bend

Savannah

Blockade

New Orleans

Pensacola

A t l a n t i c

O c e a n

500 kilometers

500 miles

Chapter One:
The March Toward War

Life in Great Britain

In the 1800s, Great Britain was one of the richest countries in the world. It was the first country to use industrial machines to make cloth and mine coal. British businesses grew quickly by importing and exporting goods. Ships sailed in and out of Great Britain's busy ports.

Great Britain is part of Europe, but there were British colonies across the world. Beginning in the 1600s, Britain and France raced each other to set up colonies in North America and India in order to become the biggest and strongest country in the world. They fought several wars to stop each other from grabbing too much power. In 1763, Britain won the Seven Years' War (1756–1763) and took France's land in North America and India. This meant that Great Britain won Canada and all the French

Great Britain Before 1812

1707 England and Scotland join to become the United Kingdom of Great Britain

1763 At the end of the Seven Years' War, Great Britain wins Canada from France

1783 Great Britain loses its American colonies in the American Revolutionary War

1801 Ireland joins Great Britain to form the United Kingdom of Great Britain and Ireland

Right: This cartoon from the early 1800s shows Emperor Napoleon of France bringing French troops by boat to threaten Britain.

territory east of the Mississippi River in present-day United States. But this victory did not end the fighting between Great Britain and France.

The Napoleonic Wars

Great Britain and France went to war again in 1792. In 1799, Napoleon Bonaparte became the dictator of France. He was hungry for power and used his army and navy to take control over as many countries as he could. He threatened to invade Great Britain several times, but the British held him off. By 1812, France controlled most of Europe, except for Great Britain and Russia.

During the Napoleonic Wars (1803–1815), Great Britain fought for its survival. Its navy was superior to France's, but Great Britain needed to keep pouring money into acquiring new ships and more sailors. It also needed to continue trading with other countries to get supplies and to raise money for its navy.

Life in Canada

France's colonies in North America were called New France. In the early 1700s, New France stretched from Labrador in present-day Canada

Below: A page from a newspaper published in 1798 in Philadelphia, Pennsylvania, shows a map of the planned French invasion of England and Ireland.

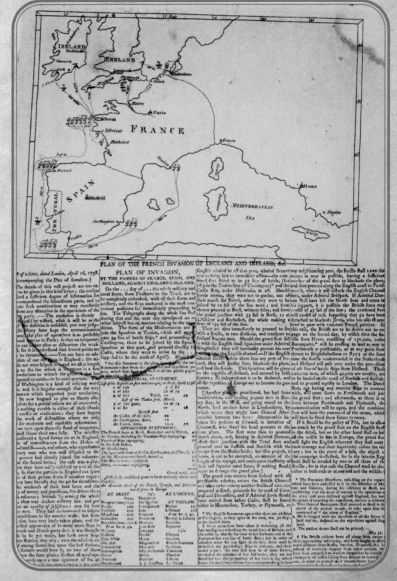

to the Gulf of Mexico in present-day Louisiana. Many towns in New France started when fur traders and trading companies set up trading posts.

While France and Great Britain fought wars in Europe, their soldiers also fought wars in their North American colonies. Both sides wanted more land and power. From 1689 to 1763, they fought four wars. In 1763, the British finally overpowered the French. The fight in North America came to an end. Great Britain took over most of New France.

By 1812, the people of what is now Canada were all British subjects. British laws governed them. They fought in Great Britain's army and navy. Many people in Canada were French Canadians. Although they were British subjects, they kept their French language, culture, and traditions.

Below: Leader of the British forces, General James Wolfe, lies dying (center) after his successful defeat of French forces at Quebec City, New France, in 1759.

Loyalists
During and after the American Revolutionary War, about 40,000 Americans moved north to settle in British North America (now Canada).

These people were called Loyalists, Royalists, or the King's Men, because they stayed loyal to Great Britain and King George III. Loyalists felt safer and more comfortable as British subjects in Canada.

Many of the Loyalists had played an important role in settling the Thirteen Colonies. They did not support the revolution against King George III. They did not believe that the new United States would succeed with its "government of the people." One Loyalist, the Reverend Mather Byles, said, "Which is better—to be ruled by one tyrant three thousand miles away [Britain] or by three thousand tyrants one mile away [the revolutionary colonists]?"

When Loyalists found themselves on the losing side of the Revolutionary War, they left their homes for Canada. They left their possessions behind and started a new life. Many spent the first months of this new life camping in the wilderness. They lived in tents until they set up communities.

Below: Some Americans hated Loyalists. This cartoon of 1783 shows patriotic colonists dressed as Native people killing a group of Loyalists.

Below: Loyalists leave the United States in 1780 to live under British rule in Canada.

Life in the United States

In 1812, the United States consisted of 18 states in the eastern part of North America. Year by year, the nation spread westward. Pioneers moved from the busy towns and seaports on the east coast to settle in the territories of Illinois, Indiana, Michigan, Mississippi, and Missouri. At the time, the United States shared the North American continent with other countries. Canada belonged to Great Britain. Florida, Texas, and some western parts of the continent belonged to Spain.

The United States was a youngster among the other nations in the world. In 1783, it won its independence from Great Britain and set up a new government. George Washington was elected the first president of the nation in 1789.

Freedom and democracy

In the early 1800s, "independence" was an important word for Americans. Families had lost sons, brothers, fathers, and cousins in the war against Great Britain. It was a big price to pay, but many Americans felt that their independence was worth it.

Population of the United States

The largest cities in the United States in 1814 were:

City	Population
New York, NY	95,519
Philadelphia, PA	92,247
Baltimore, MD	46,555
Boston, MA	33,250
Charleston, SC	27,711
New Orleans, LA	17,242

Different Everyday Concerns and Needs

The Thirteen Colonies joined together to become one nation. Still, people in different parts of the country wanted different things.

Regions of the United States	What people cared about
New England (Connecticut, Massachusetts, New Hampshire, Rhode Island, Vermont)	Shipbuilding; working at shipping docks; manufacturing; importing and exporting goods
The South (Georgia, Kentucky, North Carolina, South Carolina, Tennessee, Virginia)	Growing cotton and other crops on large plantations; maintaining slavery
Northwest Territories, also called the **West** (present-day Illinois, Indiana, Michigan, Ohio, Wisconsin, and parts of Minnesota)	Building new towns; making peace with or taking over land from Native Americans

They had won their freedom from rulers who lived across the Atlantic Ocean and set rules for Americans. They had won the freedom to make their own laws.

In the months leading up to the War of 1812, this independence from Great Britain's rules would become important all over again.

As the new nation got on its feet, it set up a democratic government. Each of the 18 states sent representatives to Congress to make laws and decisions for the country. The decisions did not come easily. People in different parts of the country wanted different things.

Below: This is a portion of the Treaty of Paris, signed on September 3, 1783. The treaty ended the Revolutionary War and gave independence to the Thirteen Colonies.

without Difficulty and without requiring any Compensation.

Article 10th.

The solemn Ratifications of the present Treaty expedited in good & due Form shall be exchanged between the contracting Parties in the Space of Six Months or sooner if possible to be computed from the Day of the Signature of the present Treaty. In Witness whereof we the undersigned their Ministers Plenipotentiary have in their Name and in Virtue of our Full Powers signed with our Hands the present Definitive Treaty, and caused the Seals of our Arms to be affix'd thereto.

Done at Paris, this third Day of September, In the Year of our Lord one thousand seven hundred and Eighty three.

Hartley John Adams. B Franklin John Jay

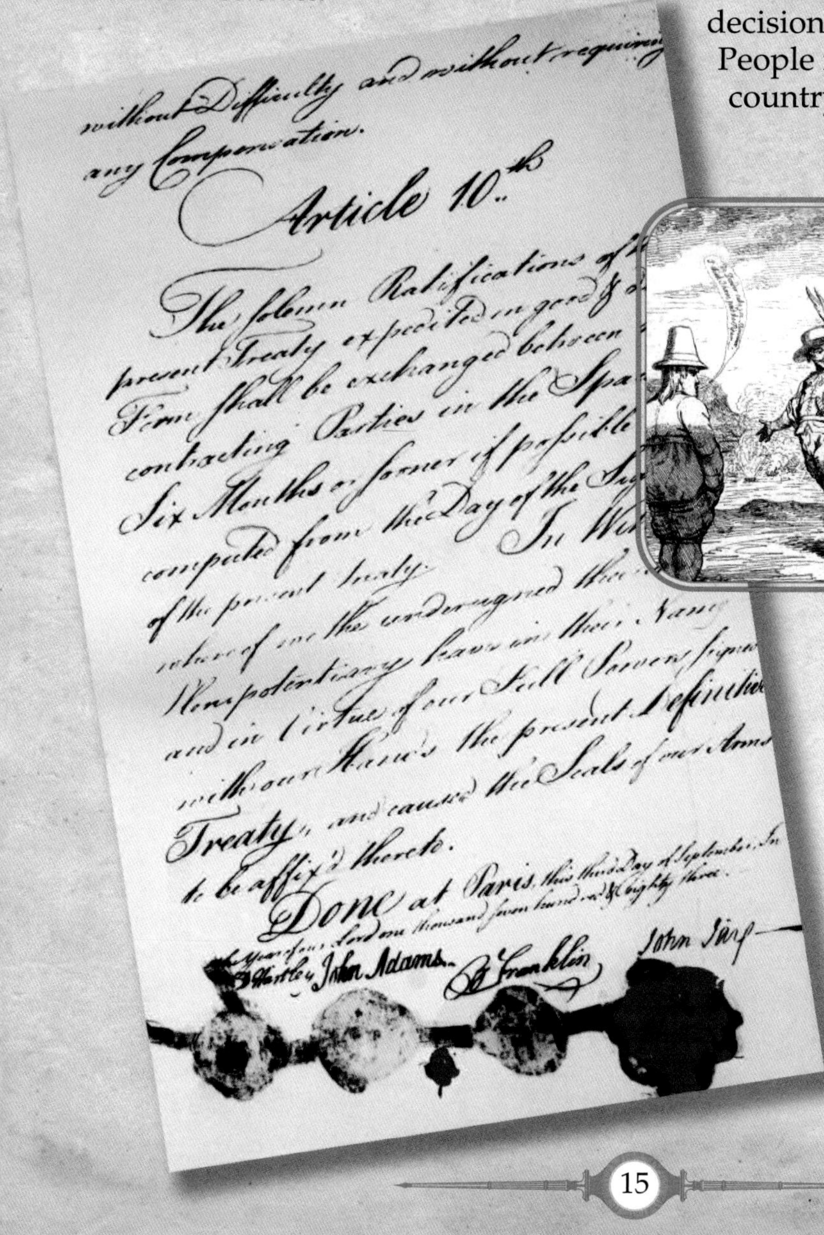

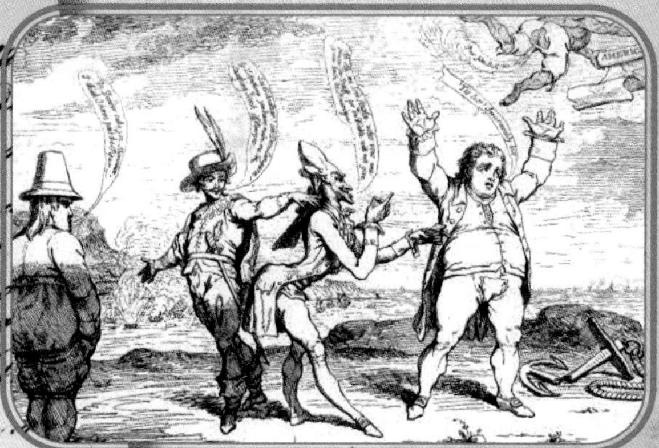

Above: A cartoon of the time showing Great Britain—symbolized by a stout, common-man character named John Bull (the figure on the right)—upset over the Treaty of Paris.

Chapter Two:
Taking Over More Land

At first the United States filled just a small part of the North American continent. In 1783, most of the nation's five million people lived within just 50 miles (80 kilometers) of the Atlantic Ocean.

Many Americans wanted to see the nation grow westward, all the way to the Pacific Ocean. Some traders and explorers made maps and brought back information about the rivers and mountains to the west, but most people knew little of these lands. They also knew little about the homelands, customs, and traditions of the thousands of Native North Americans who had lived in these lands for centuries.

Below: As Americans settled the frontier, they came into conflict with Native North American warriors.

Growing challenges

As the new nation grew, it faced many challenges. Great Britain continued to be a problem. Although the American Revolutionary War had forced the British out of their American colonies, there were still fierce arguments about the border between British-owned Canada and the United States. Even though the Treaty of Paris of 1783 ordered the British out of their military posts in Michigan, New York, and Ohio, the British did not hurry to leave because the United States had not honored some of the terms of the treaty.

British traders used their forts as trading posts with the Native people. The Wyandots, Delawares, Shawnees, Chippawas, and other Native people knew the forests well and trapped beavers, mink, and raccoons there. They traded these furs to European traders for goods such as guns, blankets, tools, and alcohol. The furs brought high prices in European markets.

Above: A fur trader does business with a group of Native North Americans.

A common enemy
In addition to enjoying the fur trade, Great Britain kept friendships with the Native North Americans for other reasons. Great Britain wanted to protect Canada from attacks by the United States. The British encouraged Native people to join them in keeping out U.S. troops. Sometimes the British gave them guns. They used these guns to protect their own land from white settlers. As Americans tried to settle the Northwest Territory, they often came into conflict with Native people armed with British weapons.

Tecumseh and the Prophet

Several Native leaders made treaties with the Americans even when many of them did not represent their nations and had no authority to trade away their lands. Two Shawnee leaders, Tecumseh and his brother, the Prophet, tried to encourage their people and other nations, including the Creek, Kickapoo, Menominee, and Osage, to band together to hold on to their land. William Henry Harrison, the governor of Indiana Territory, sent this message to the two leaders:

"Don't deceive yourselves; do not believe that all the nations of Indians united are able to resist the force of the Seventeen Fires [the then 17 states of the United States]. I know your warriors are brave, but ours are not less so; but what can a few brave warriors do, against the innumerable warriors of the Seventeen Fires? Our blue coats are more numerous than you can

Below: William Henry Harrison took command of the U.S. Army of the Northwest in September of 1812. Here, he is shown fighting at Tippecanoe in 1811.

count; our hunters are like the leaves of the forest, or the grains of sand on the Wabash. Do not think that the red coats [British] can protect you; they are not able to protect themselves. They do not think of going to war with us. If they did, you would in a few moons see our flag wave over all the forts of Canada."

The Prophet sent back this reply:

"The Great Spirit gave this great island to his red children; he placed the whites on the other side of the big water; they were not contented with their own, but came to take ours from us. They have driven us from the sea to the lakes: we can go no further."

Below: Harrison's army defeated the Native warriors at the Battle of Tippecanoe.

The Battle of Tippecanoe

In 1808, Tecumseh and the Prophet set up the village named Prophetstown in Indiana, near the Tippecanoe and Wabash Rivers (present-day Vincennes). In 1811, an angry Governor Harrison sent 1,100 men to camp outside the village. The Prophet gathered a band of 600 followers to attack Harrison's troops. After three attacks, the Prophet's men ran out of ammunition. Harrison's troops drove them out and burned the village to the ground. Harrison became a hero for winning the Battle of Tippecanoe. In 1840, Americans elected him president of the United States.

Doubling in size

In 1802, France owned the vast area of North America from the Mississippi River to the Rocky Mountains. It was called Louisiana. It captured the interest of Americans for two reasons. First, many Americans, including President Thomas Jefferson, wanted the nation to grow from sea to sea. The purchase of Louisiana would bring that goal closer. Second, Americans wanted to be sure they could use the port of New Orleans. Farmers near the Mississippi River sent their crops down the river to New Orleans, into the Gulf of Mexico, and out to ports by the Atlantic Ocean. President Jefferson was afraid that France might stop letting Americans use this port.

Jefferson first offered to buy only New Orleans from France. Before the deal was finished, however, he managed to buy all of Louisiana for $15 million. Today that sum is worth about $269 million. The U.S. Senate approved the deal, and the United States doubled in size. Thirteen new states were eventually carved out of Louisiana: Arkansas, Colorado, Iowa, Kansas, Louisiana, Minnesota, Missouri, Montana, Nebraska, North Dakota, Oklahoma, South Dakota, and Wyoming.

Above: This portrait of President Thomas Jefferson was painted in 1801.

Left: By 1812, the capital of the United States was Washington, D.C. Leaders made important decisions for the nation here.

Right: This treaty between the United States and France spelled out the terms of the Louisiana Purchase.

(Original)

Treaty

Between the United States of America and the French Republic

The President of the United States of America and the First Consul of the French Republic in the name of the French People desiring to remove all Source of misunderstanding relative to objects of discussion mentioned in the Second and fifth articles of the Convention of the { 8th Vendémiaire an 9 / 30 September 1800 } relative to the rights claimed by the United States in virtue of the Treaty concluded at Madrid the 27 of October 1795, between His Catholic Majesty, & the Said United States, & willing to Strengthen the union and friendship which at the time of the Said Convention was happily reestablished between the two nations have respectively named their Plenipotentiaries to wit The President of the United States, by and with the advice and consent of the Senate of the Said State; Robert R. Livingston Minister Plenipotentiary of the United State and James Monroe Minister Plenipotentiary and Envoy extraordinary of the Said State near the Government of the French Republic; And the First Consul in the name of the French people, Citizen Francis Barbé Marbois Minister of the public treasury who after having respectively exchanged their full powers have agreed to the following articles

Remove the British for good!

Many Americans thought that they could not fill the continent with new roads and towns until the British left for good. Americans believed that Great Britain was helping the Native North Americans keep out the white settlers. They felt it was time for Great Britain to honor America's independence and stay out of its business. In Congress in 1811, representative Felix Grundy of Tennessee said:

> "We shall drive the British from our continent—they will no longer have an opportunity of intriguing with our Indian neighbors, and setting on the ruthless savage to tomahawk our women and children. That nation will lose her Canadian trade, and, by having no resting place in this country, her means of annoying us will be diminished."

Above: As Americans moved into the Northwest Territory, they traveled by covered wagons on dirt trails.

Did the United States want to take over Canada, too? Congressman John Randolph from Virginia suggested this in 1811 and others in Congress, particularly the War Hawks, agreed. Some thought it might be good to conquer Upper Canada and then trade it for peace on the seas.

Chapter Three: "A Free Trade and Sailors' Rights"

One of the most important reasons why the United States declared war was the British threat to its freedom on the seas. As part of their strategy for defeating Napoleon, the British prevented neutral countries from trading with France and with its allies. If ships cannot sail to and from ports, people stop buying and selling goods. Businesses stop earning money.

Prospering from Europe's war

At first, Great Britain's war with France was good news for Americans. Great Britain and France stopped trading with each other. U.S. merchants, farmers, and storekeepers grew richer as the war continued. The United States was a neutral country and so did not favor either side.

Below: New Orleans, Louisiana, was an important shipping port in the early 1800s.

Above: The Battle of Trafalgar in 1805

It shipped profitably to France and Great Britain, as well as other countries drawn into the war such as Spain, Austria, Prussia, and Russia. The United States quickly became the country with the largest neutral trade in the world. Between 1803 and 1805, U.S. trade grew three times larger. U.S. shipbuilders built more ships, farmers sold more crops, and lumberyards sold more lumber.

Trouble at sea

This good fortune for the United States did not last. Great Britain and France decided to cut off each other's trade. First, France issued the Berlin Decree of 1806 in an attempt to stop all trade ships going to Great Britain. Then, Great Britain passed its own Orders-in-Council in an attempt to stop all trade ships going to France and its allies.

The British Navy

The British Royal Navy was one of the most powerful in the world. In the Battle of Trafalgar, off the coast of Spain, Britain's 27 ships defeated 33 French and Spanish ships. Admiral Lord Nelson lined up his fleet in two columns to attack the enemy. He died in battle and became one of Great Britain's greatest war heroes.

Above: In 1812 and 1813, Britain sent ships to blockade the American coastline.

Both countries set up blockades, which meant sending ships to block each other's ports. American merchant ships were having a hard time reaching either country.

In 1807, the U.S. Congress passed an Embargo Act which prevented Americans from trading with France and Great Britain, hoping this would stop the blockades since both countries relied on U.S. goods. Hundreds of U.S. ships were stopped. In the end, the embargo was not successful and only served to hurt the economy of the United States.

Seizure and impressment

Blockades were not the only problem on the seas. Further trouble came when Great Britain and France began capturing American merchant vessels. Between 1803 and 1812, Great Britain and France each seized about 850 ships. Even when the ships were released, the owners lost time and money.

Running the Blockade

During the War of 1812, British ships blockaded U.S. ports. Some adventurous U.S. captains chose to try to run their ships right through the blockades. There was lots of money to be made by transporting products to ports that greatly needed them. The risk was great. These private ships could have been fired upon. The sailors could have been captured and forced to serve in the British Navy. Still, many ships successfully sailed through the blockades.

Left: A U.S. sailor is impressed by a British Navy captain and his men.

Aside from stopping the ships, the British also captured sailors to serve in its navy. This was called impressment. Why did Great Britain impress sailors? The war with France was wearing down the British Royal Navy. After nearly 20 years of nonstop fighting, it was difficult to staff a navy that had more than 580 ships and 114,000 sailors. It was hard to get volunteers for a job that was extremely dangerous and paid very little. Thousands of British sailors ran away from this job. Many looked for work on private ships or in the navies of other countries.

A fight for rights

British officers searched towns and ports for sailors who had deserted, or run away, from the Royal Navy. They stopped ships at sea including many U.S. ships. There were, in fact, British sailors on U.S. ships. Some had joined the U.S. ships to earn more money.

Below: American sailors were taken from their ships and forced to fight for the British Royal Navy.

Below: An angry article from a Boston newspaper of March 25, 1808 blasts the boarding of U.S. ships.

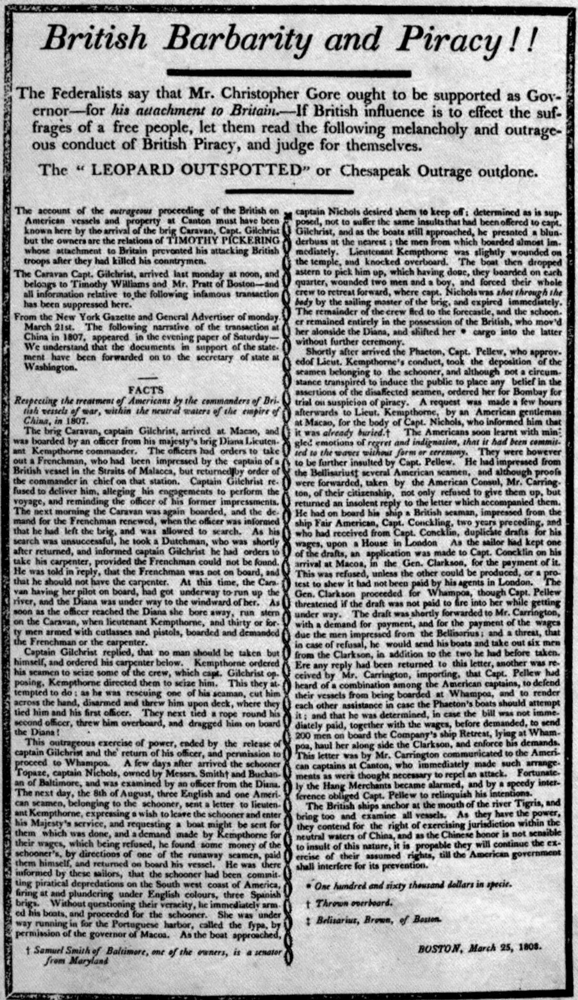

Others had moved to the United States but had not yet become U.S. citizens. In the fury of taking back British sailors, many British-born American sailors were captured, too. The British believed that a person owed allegiance to their country of birth even though they had become a citizen of another country such as the United States. British officers took deserters from the Royal Navy off American ships and punished them and forced them to continue service in the Royal Navy. Mistakes were made, and some deserters were kept in prison for years. Some historians estimate that the British impressed 5,000 legitimate U.S. citizens between 1793 and 1812 but most of these men were released when their citizenship was proven. In 1812, many angry Americans chanted the slogan: "A free trade and sailors' rights."

In January 27, 1812, an impressed sailor named Shepard Bourne sent this letter. Some of the misspellings and punctuation have been changed.

Dear Mother,
I am sorry to inform you that I have the misfortune to be impressed in the British service and am now on board the San Juan lying at the Rock of Gibraltar. I hope that you can make my case now to Major Cousins and use your endeavors to get me discharged as soon as possible as I am very anxious to get home to my wife and family if not to you. When I was in Quebec the 11th of last June I had the misfortune to be impressed shortly afterward and have no likely modes of getting clear without the assistance of you. I hope these few lines will find you and all my family in good health as I am at present.

British Barbarity and Piracy!!

The Federalists say that Mr. Christopher Gore ought to be supported as Governor—for *his attachment to Britain.*—If British influence is to effect the suffrages of a free people, let them read the following melancholy and outrageous conduct of British Piracy, and judge for themselves.

The "LEOPARD OUTSPOTTED" or Chesapeak Outrage outdone.

[newspaper article text, partially legible]

BOSTON, March 25, 1808.

A British attack

In the spring of 1807, the U.S. Navy frigate U.S.S. *Chesapeake* sailed off the coast of Norfolk, Virginia. Many of the *Chesapeake*'s sailors were British. On June 22, the British frigate H.M.S. *Leopard* approached the *Chesapeake*. The British commander, Salusbury Pryce Humphreys, requested to board the *Chesapeake* and search for British deserters. The *Chesapeake*'s captain, James Barron, refused. Sailors on the *Leopard* fired at the *Chesapeake*, killing three and wounding 16. Then they boarded the *Chesapeake* and removed four men. Three of them turned out to be American citizens; only one was a Royal Navy deserter. He was hanged.

In 1811, Great Britain apologized to the United States for the attack. Americans were outraged by the incident. Some members of Congress began to call for war.

Above: A British Navy officer from H.M.S. *Leopard* confronts the crew of the *Chesapeake* as he searches for deserters.

Chapter Four: Debating the War

Should the United States declare war on Great Britain? People in Great Britain and what is now Canada thought: "Definitely not!" Great Britain had enough problems in the war with France. Anne Prevost, the daughter of the governor of Lower Canada, summed up the emotions of British subjects when she wrote in her diary on June 25, 1812:

"This war was a base deed on the part of the Yankees [Americans]. England was struggling for her independence against a host of foes, and the United States chose that moment to add their vile kicks and cuffs, hoping the Noble Lion was sinking in the fray, overwhelmed by numbers."

Below: This picture from the time shows an empty warehouse on a wharf in Portland, Maine. The 1807 embargo had stopped all shipping to this port.

Different viewpoints

Did Americans want to go to war over "free trade and sailors' rights"? Not all of them did. It depended who the Americans were and where they lived.

Most of the people in the states along the northeastern coast wanted to take all necessary steps to avoid going to war. Many earned their living in shipping and trading. France and Great Britain's harsh shipping rules made life difficult, but a war would surely be worse.

In the South and West, many people were ready for war. They wanted to send the British away for good. Many of these Americans were farmers who depended on the land. Those with large farms needed to ship their crops to sell in other places. Others wanted to spread out across the West, while others wanted to annex Upper Canada and lands west of that province. And if Great Britain kept helping the Native people with guns and other

Above: Farmers such as these in Cranbury, New Jersey, in 1810, had too much to lose by going to war with Great Britain.

Above: The artist of this cartoon shows Americans' anger at the Embargo (O-grab-me spelled backward) Act of 1807.

supplies, white settlers could not take over new land for their farms and towns. This also angered many Americans.

Political parties

When the United States became independent, there were no political parties. By 1789, there were two: Federalists and Republicans (also called Democratic–Republicans). Federalists included wealthy merchants and business owners. They wanted to keep the economy strong and build a strong army and navy.

The Republicans felt that small state militias would, if necessary, protect the country. Thomas Jefferson was the first Republican president. He shrunk the size of the army and stopped the building of naval ships. Many wondered what would happen if the country went to war.

Jefferson stops shipping

Thomas Jefferson was president from 1801 to 1809. Like presidents Washington and Adams before him, Jefferson wanted to avoid war. The United States was still young and its navy was no match for Great Britain's. To avoid war in late 1807, Jefferson asked Congress to pass the Embargo Act. An embargo is a ban on trade with another country. This law stopped all trade between the United States and other countries. Jefferson thought it would starve the British and French of goods and money. This would make them stop interfering with U.S. trade.

Jefferson was wrong. The Embargo Act hurt Americans most of all. Farmers could not sell their crops. Merchants could not sell their goods. Ship owners and sailors lost their jobs. Americans could not buy sugar, salt, tea, and other goods imported from other countries. Finally, in 1809, Congress ended the Embargo Act and replaced it with the

The Importance of Shipping

This chart shows the value of goods that were imported and exported to and from the United States.

Exports
1790	$20,000,000
1807	$108,000,000

Imports
1790	$23,000,000
1807	$139,000,000

Below: In this cartoon of 1808, President Jefferson defends his Embargo Act to a group of citizens who disagree.

Non-Intercourse Act. This act allowed Americans to trade with all nations except France and Great Britain. If either France or Great Britain stopped seizing ships and sailors, the United States would start trading with them again. By 1810, France promised to respect the rights of U.S. ships. Great Britain would not make such a promise. However, some American merchants defied their own country and continued to bring supplies to the British throughout the embargo and war.

The War Hawks

James Madison became president in 1809. Like Jefferson, he was a Republican and hoped to stop Great Britain's interference in a peaceful way. But Great Britain showed no signs of ending its interference with U.S. shipping. Many Republicans in Congress called for war. The Federalists nicknamed these congressmen "War Hawks."

In Congress, the War Hawks argued three reasons to declare war with Great Britain and invade Canada. First: To stop Great Britain's Orders-in-Council, which seriously interfered with U.S. trade, and stop the impressment of sailors from American trading ships.

Below: Rich merchants, such as Timothy Dexter who lived in this house in Newburyport, Massachusetts, until 1806, did not want to risk losing their wealth. Dexter displayed his wealth by erecting 40 wooden statues of famous men, including George Washington, Thomas Jefferson, and Napoleon Bonaparte.

Second: To stop the British from encouraging Native people to attack new American settlements in the Northwest Territory. Third: To remind Great Britain and the world that the United States won its independence in 1783. The United States must defend its right to freedom.

The War Hawks felt sure that victory would be easy. While Great Britain had many ships, it did not have enough soldiers to defend its land in Canada. The United States could send its troops over the border and easily take over Upper Canada. The annexation would take away the British Indian Department headquarters where British agents forged alliances with Native nations. It could also be used as a bargaining chip to stop Britain's interference in shipping.

Below: James Madison was president of the United States from 1809 to 1817.

Chapter Five:
Were They Ready for War?

Gradually, the War Hawks gained support. On June 1, 1812, President Madison finally gave in. He asked Congress to declare war on Great Britain. All the Federalists in Congress objected to war, but more and more Republicans accepted the idea. Some, however, hoped that Great Britain would back down even before the fighting began.

Great Britain's leaders tried to calm the situation. They did not want to fight another war while the war with France was still raging. Great Britain had lost 290,000 troops since 1789. It could not spare the soldiers nor the ships for a war in North America.

Below: A British cartoon from 1812 sends "a bad news for you" message to President Madison. This appeared after U.S. troops surrendered Detroit and the territory of Michigan. The two women stand for Britain (on the left, with a lion) and the United States (shown as a Native American).

Who Supported the War?

For the votes in Congress in June 1812, there was a majority decision in favor of the war in both the Senate and the House of Representatives.

For the War	Against the War
War Hawks in the **Republican** Party	**Federalists**
States in the South and West (less affected by interference in shipping; wanted to invade Canada and stop Great Britain from helping Native Americans who were stopping the progress of settlers)	**States in the Northeast** (depended on manufacturing and shipping; afraid to lose trade)
Vote in Congress: Senate – **19** House – **79**	**Vote in Congress:** Senate – **13** House – **49**

Great Britain cancels the Orders-in-Council

On June 16, 1812—just two days before Congress would take their war vote—Lord Castlereagh, the British Foreign Secretary, made an announcement that he thought would change everything. Great Britain would cancel the Orders-in-Council. This did not stop the war, however, as the announcement took at least five weeks to cross the Atlantic Ocean.

The news traveled by ship and did not reach Congress before they voted. It was the closest vote on any formal declaration of war in American history. The United States declared war on Great Britain on June 18, 1812.

Could speedier communications have avoided a war? We will never know. Some historians feel that unless the British gave up impressment as well as the Orders-in-Council, the war was unavoidable. Also, the desire by many of the War Hawks to capture Upper Canada had become too strong.

Great Britain prepares for war

Great Britain was one of the world's strongest powers, but its soldiers and ships were busy fighting

Madison on the War

Although President Madison tried to avoid war, he saw no other option. In his first message to Congress after the war began, he said that if the United States had avoided war, it:

"would have acknowledged that on [water] … where all independent nations have equal and common rights, the American people were not an independent people but colonists and vassals."

France in Europe. It could not spare soldiers to send to British North America. At the time, Great Britain had only 6,000 troops there. They would need local help. Would the Canadians be helpful? In New Brunswick and Nova Scotia, about 60,000 people could be counted on as strong British supporters. Great Britain also hoped for the support of its native friends in the Kickapoo, Menominee, Shawnee, and Winnebago nations. In Lower Canada most people (about 200,000) were French and while some British questioned whether or not they would defend their land against American invasions, history proved them to be loyal supporters of the British. In Upper Canada more than half of the total population of 60,000 were American immigrants who had come in the past two decades. Nonetheless, these new subjects of the Crown proved every bit as willing to defend Upper Canada against their former countrymen. All things considered, there were as many as 50,000 British North American men who were eligible to volunteer for military service. In the United States there were more than 600,000 men who could oppose them.

Below: This 1813 cartoon makes fun of soldiers from New York State who are marching to Buffalo to help the U.S. side in the war. The artist was William Charles.

Below: Americans could read President Madison's official declaration of war in this Philadelphia, Pennsylvania, newspaper article.

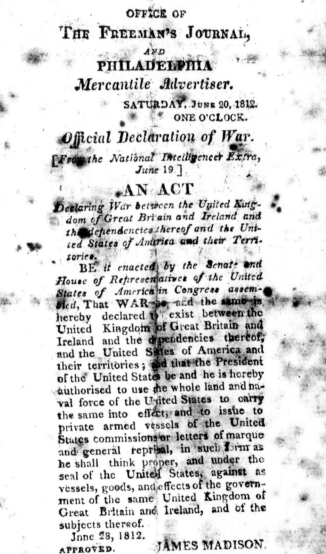

OFFICE OF

THE FREEMAN'S JOURNAL,

AND

PHILADELPHIA

Mercantile Advertiser.

SATURDAY, JUNE 20, 1812.
ONE O'CLOCK.

Official Declaration of War.

[From the National Intelligencer Extra, June 19.]

AN ACT

Declaring War between the United Kingdom of Great Britain and Ireland and the dependencies thereof and the United States of America and their Territories.

BE it enacted by the Senate and House of Representatives of the United States of America in Congress assembled, That WAR be and the same is hereby declared to exist between the United Kingdom of Great Britain and Ireland and the dependencies thereof, and the United States of America and their territories; and that the President of the United States be and he is hereby authorised to use the whole land and naval force of the United States to carry the same into effect; and to issue to private armed vessels of the United States commissions or letters of marque and general reprisal, in such form as he shall think proper, and under the seal of the United States, against as vessels, goods, and effects of the government of the same United Kingdom of Great Britain and Ireland, and of the subjects thereof.

June 28, 1812.
APPROVED.   JAMES MADISON.

[Subscribers are requested to call at the Office for this Supplement.]

Canada prepares for war

The number of British North Americans who were fit to fight was limited as were weapons and other military supplies. However, Canada had two strong military leaders, George Prevost and Isaac Brock. These two British military men did not agree on how they would fight the war. Prevost had been ordered to remain on the defensive in hopes that the Americans would remain divided on fighting the war. The British also knew that they had to conserve their

Below: A painting shows U.S. Commodore Oliver Hazard Perry standing in a small boat after abandoning his flagship, the U.S.S. *Lawrence.*

limited troops and supplies to make sure that Quebec City could be defended. Brock, on the other hand, wanted to attack the Americans whenever the opportunity arose.

The United States prepares for war

When the United States declared war, people in the South and West marched in parades and signed up to serve in the army. However, the mood was different in New England. In Hartford, Connecticut, people felt so sad that they lowered their flags as a sign of mourning. Connecticut and Massachusetts at first refused to send any soldiers for this war. Some people wanted their states to leave the United States. This desire did not disappear. At the Hartford Convention in late 1814, the representatives of the states of Connecticut, Massachusetts, New Hampshire, and Rhode Island talked about leaving the Union if the war continued. They did not leave, but the war was soon brought to an end.

Below: The war continued into 1815. This picture shows the Battle of New Orleans, fought after the signing of the Treaty of Ghent.

GLOSSARY

allies Nations that are on the same side of a war

American Revolutionary War The war between Great Britain and its 13 American colonies from 1775 to 1783

army A large group of people trained to fight on land

Berlin Decree Orders from Napoleon, ruler of France, to stop all trading with Great Britain and to blockade British ports

blockade Shutting off a port to keep ships from bringing in or taking out goods

boarding party Sailors that board an enemy ship to capture it or board a merchant ship to impress sailors

border Dividing line between two countries

colony A place where people live far from the country that rules it. The original 13 U.S. states were once British colonies.

Congress In the United States, two groups of representatives who make laws for the nation; the two groups are the Senate and the House of Representatives

defensive Trying to defend or protect yourself or your group

democracy A form of government based on rule by the people, usually through their elected representatives

deserter Someone who runs away, usually from the army or navy

dictator A leader who takes all the power in a country

document An official or original paper such as a letter, newspaper, or treaty, but also items that serve as proof or evidence, for example, a painting, photograph, engraving, or poster

embargo A government order forbidding trade with another country

export To send goods to another country to sell

fleet A group of ships in a country's navy

free trade Trade between nations without interference, such as tariffs or taxes, from government

frigate Mid-size warship used during the 1800s

import To bring in goods from another country to sell

impress To force people to serve as sailors or soldiers

interfere To get in the way; to stop or prevent

Loyalist An American who stayed loyal or friendly to Great Britain during the Revolution

merchant A person who earns money by trading or selling items

militia An army of private citizens organized to defend their country

Napoleonic Wars A series of conflicts between France (led by Napoleon) and other European countries that lasted from 1803 to 1815

national anthem A song of loyalty to one's country

Native North American An original inhabitant of North America before the continent was settled by Europeans; sometimes referred to as American Indians, Native Americans, or First Nations people

navy A country's military sea force, including ships and people

negotiations Meetings and discussions between two or more opposing sides with the goal of coming to an agreement

neutral Choosing not to fight or ally with any side of a war

Northwest Territory In the United States, land that was being settled in the 1790s. It included present-day Illinois, Indiana, Michigan, Ohio, Wisconsin, and parts of Minnesota.

Orders-in-Council Before the War of 1812, laws set by Britain to forbid and block neutral countries from trading with France or its allies

patriotic Loyal to one's country; a patriot is someone who is patriotic

political party A group that is organized to promote certain policies and leaders in government

port A town or city by the water where ships load and unload goods and passengers

president The elected head of the U.S. government

recruit To convince someone to join the army or navy

representative Someone who acts or speaks for people as laws are made and amended

Seven Years' War Conflicts from 1756 to 1763 in which European countries fought for dominance; Britain and France also fought for control of the seas and land in North America from 1754 to 1760

shipyard A place where ships are built and repaired

slavery One person owning another person and making that person do work, without pay

territory In the United States, an area that is not yet a state

Thirteen Colonies Britain's colonies in North America that eventually won independence and formed the first United States of America. The colonies were, in order of founding: Virginia, Massachusetts, New Hampshire, Maryland, Connecticut, Rhode Island, Delaware, North Carolina, South Carolina, New Jersey, New York, Pennsylvania, and Georgia.

trading post Place where people meet to trade goods

treason The crime of helping the enemy or being disloyal to one's own country

treaty Written agreement between two countries, usually to prevent or end a war

volunteer Offer to do a job instead of being commanded to do it

War Hawk Congressman from the South and West who wanted to go to war with Britain in 1812

CHRONOLOGY

1763
Great Britain wins the Seven Years' War and takes over France's land in North America, including colonies in Canada.

1783
The United States wins the American Revolutionary War, ending Great Britain's rule over its 13 American colonies.

1792
Britain and Revolutionary France at war.

1799
Napoleon Bonaparte becomes the dictator of France and has ambitions of expanding his empire in Europe. This brings France into conflict again with Great Britain.

1801
Peace of Amiens temporarily ends the war between Britain and France.

1803
The United States buys Louisiana from France and doubles in size.
Napoleonic Wars flare up again that will last until 1815.

1805
October 21 British Navy destroys French and its Spanish ally's ships at the Battle of Trafalgar.

1806
France issues the Berlin Decree to stop trade going to Great Britain.

1807
Great Britain's Orders-in-Council ban neutral countries from trading with France.
France and Great Britain blockade each other's ports.
The British ship *Leopard* seizes the American *Chesapeake*.
The United States passes the Embargo Act banning U.S. trade with other countries.

1809
The United States replaces the Embargo Act with the Non-Intercourse Act banning U.S. trade with Great Britain and France until they stop their interference.

1811
In the Battle of Tippecanoe, William Henry Harrison's troops drive out the Shawnees and others while destroying the Prophetstown village.

1812
June 16 Great Britain ends the Orders-in-Council that ban trading.
June 18 President Madison signs a declaration of war on Great Britain.

MORE INFORMATION

Greenblatt, Miriam. *The War of 1812*. New York: Facts On File, Inc., 2003.

O'Neill, Robert and Carl Benn. *The War of 1812: The Fight for American Trade Rights*. New York: Rosen Publishing Group, Inc., 2011.

Raatma, Lucia. *The War of 1812*. Minneapolis: Compass Point Books, 2005.

Sonneborn, Liz. *The War of 1812: A Primary Source History of America's Second War with Britain*. New York: Rosen Publishing Group, Inc., 2004.

Zimmerman, Dwight Jon. *Tecumseh: Shooting Star of the Shawnee*. New York: Sterling, 2010.

DVDs

History Channel Presents: The War of 1812 DVD Set This two-disc collection covers the involvement and achievements of the United States in the war.

War of 1812 This four-part documentary series from the National Film Board of Canada provides a Canadian perspective on the war

WEBSITES

"Americans and British Face Off in the War of 1812" (videoclip)

www.history.com/videos/james-madison-and-the-war-of-1812#americans-and -british-face-off-in-war-of-1812

Encountering the First American West. Library of Congress

http://memory.loc.gov/ammem/award99/icuhtml/fawsp/fawsp.html

President Madison's War Message:

www.edsitement.neh.gov/curriculum-unit/president-madisons-1812-war-message

Reminiscences of Niagara. *Niagara History Society*, No 11

http://images.ourontario.ca/Partners/nhsm/NHSM0571591T.pdf

Tippecanoe Battlefield History. Tippecanoe County Historical Association

www.tcha.mus.in.us/battlehistory.htm

The U.S.S. *Chesapeake*

www.theusschesapeake.com/Home_Page.html

The War of 1812 website

http://warof1812.ca

BIBLIOGRAPHY

The following books and websites were used as the sources of primary evidence:

Introduction

    http://www.history.com/videos/james-madison-and-the-war-of-1812#americans-and-british-face-off-in-war-of-1812

The March Toward War

    Isaac Brock quote: http://images.ourontario.ca/Partners/nhsm/NHSM0571591T.pdf

    U.S. city populations: Hunt, Gaillard. *As We Were: Life in America 1814*. Stockbridge, MA: Berkshire House Publishers, 1993, p. 22.

Taking Over More Land

    Harrison and Tecumseh quotes: Found at: http://www.warof1812-history.com/life-of-tecumseh-pg-1.aspx

    Felix Grundy quote: Found at: http://memory.loc.gov/cgi-bin/ampage

"A Free Trade and Sailors' Rights"

    Horatio Nelson quote: Marcus, G.J. The Age of Nelson: The Royal Navy in the Age of Its Greatest Power and Glory, 1793-1815. New York: Viking, 1971, p. 23.

    Shepard Bourne letter: Bolster, W. Jeffrey. *Letters by African American Sailors 1799-1814*. William and Mary Quarterly, Vol. 64 (2007), p. 179.

    Expression: "Free Trade and Sailors' Rights": Found at: http://www.britannica.com/bps/additionalcontent/18/47776537/Free-Trade-and-Sailors-Rights-The-Rhetoric-of-the-War-of-1812

    Trade facts: Purcell, Sarah J. *The Early National Period*. New York: Facts On File, Inc., 2004, pp. 155–156.

    Running the blockade: http://ctatwar.cslib.org/wp-content/uploads/2010/09/Radune.pdf.

    Hickey, Donald R. *Don't Give Up the Ship: Myths of the War of 1812*. Champaign, IL: University of Illinois Press, 2006.

Debating the War

    Anne Prevost quote: Found at: http://www.uppercanadahistory.ca/1812/18121.html

    Henry Clay quote: Found at: http://memory.loc.gov/cgi-bin/ampage?collId=llac&fileName=020/llac020.db&recNum=285

Were They Ready for War?

    Madison's first wartime message to Congress: Found at: http://vftonline.org/EndTheWall/madison2.htm

    John Calhoun quote: Found at: http://www.presidentprofiles.com/Washington-Johnson/James-Madison-Madison-as-president-the-road-to-war.html

    Isaac Brock's letter of response: http://en.wikisource.org/wiki/Letter_in_Response_to_the_Declaration_of_War

    "Ye Parliament of England": *Ballads Migrant in New England*, Helen H. Flanders and Marguerite Olney, eds., New York, 1953.

    Closest vote on declaration of war: Hickey, Donald R. p. 42.

    Statistics on Senate and House vote: http://ctatwar.cslib.org/wp-content/uploads/2010/09/Radune.pdf

INDEX